Jr. Graphic Colonial

The Life of
Wigmaker

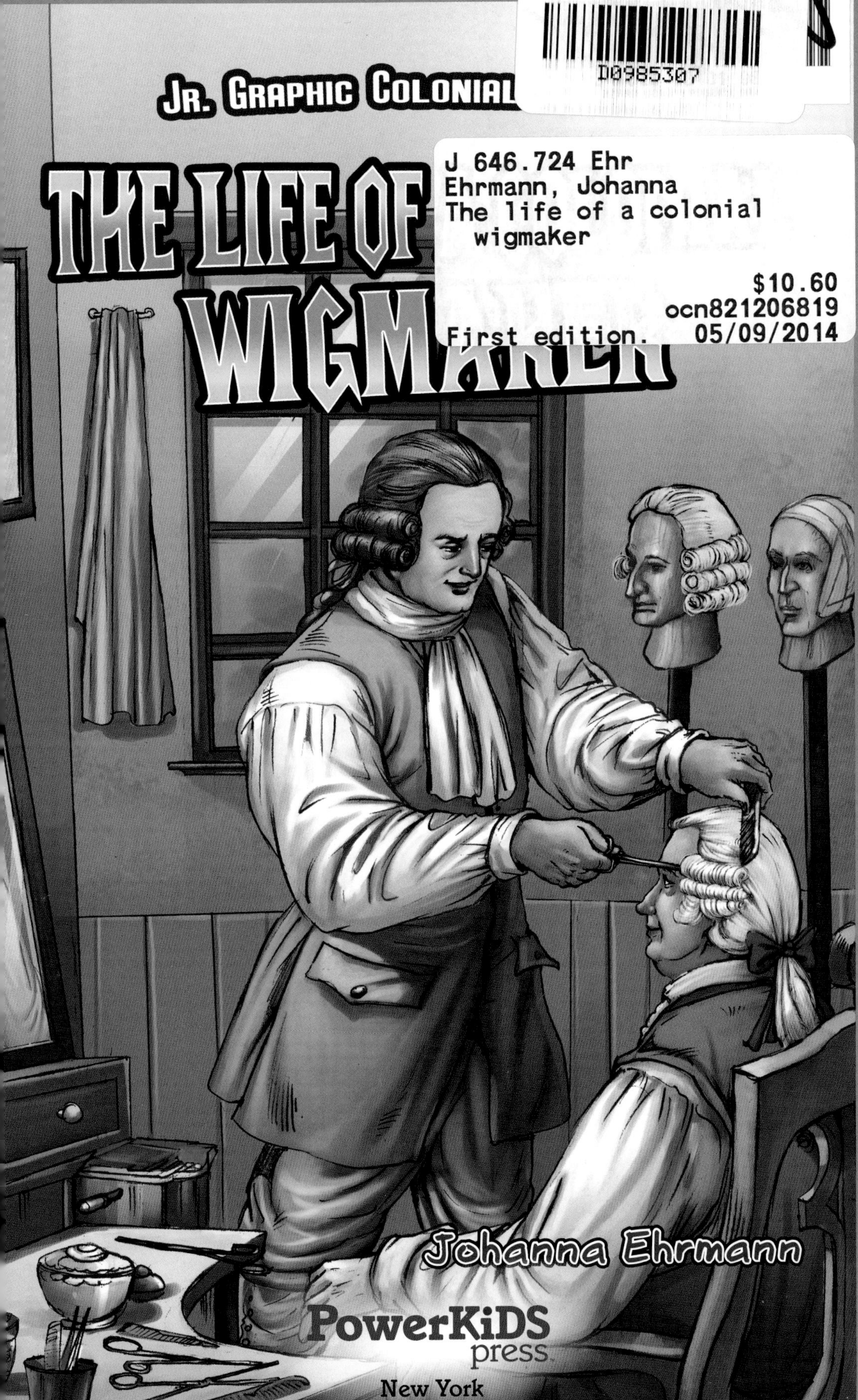

Johanna Ehrmann

PowerKiDS press
New York

Published in 2014 by The Rosen Publishing Group, Inc.
29 East 21st Street, New York, NY 10010

Note: The main characters in this book were real-life colonists who held the jobs described. In some cases, not much else is known about their lives. When necessary, we have used the best available historical scholarship on the professions and daily life in colonial America to create as full and accurate a portrayal as possible.

First Edition

Editor: Joanne Randolph
Book Design: Planman Technologies
Illustrations: Planman Technologies

Library of Congress Cataloging-in-Publication Data

Ehrmann, Johanna.
The life of a colonial wigmaker / by Johanna Ehrmann. — First edition.
     pages cm. — (Jr. graphic colonial America)
Includes index.
ISBN 978-1-4777-1307-5 (library binding) — ISBN 978-1-4777-1431-7 (pbk.) — ISBN 978-1-4777-1432-4 (6-pack)
1. Wigs—United States—History—18th century—Juvenile literature.
2. Wigmakers—United States—History—18th century—Juvenile literature.
3. Wigs—United States—History—18th century—Comic books, strips, etc.
4. Wigmakers—United States—History—18th century—Comic books, strips, etc.
5. Graphic novels. I. Title.
TT975.E37 2014
646.7'24809—dc23
                                        2012049055

Manufactured in the United States of America
CPSIA Compliance Information: Batch #S13PK1: For Further Information contact Rosen Publishing, New York, New York at 1-800-237-9932

CONTENTS

INTRODUCTION

For a man living in a town in colonial America during the 1700s, wearing a wig was a key aspect of being well **dressed**. Wigs needed upkeep to look fresh, and that took time and effort. Wigmakers, such as Edward Charlton, who operated a shop on Duke of Gloucester Street in Williamsburg, Virginia, offered many services to people who could afford them.

MAIN CHARACTERS

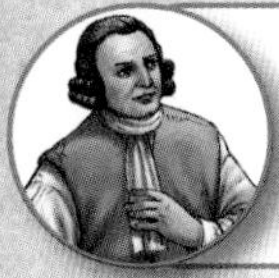

Edward Charlton (unknown–1792) A successful barber and wigmaker living in Williamsburg, Virginia, in the 1700s.

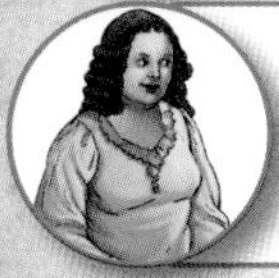

Jane Hunter Charlton (c. 1746–1802) The wife of Edward Charlton. She is a successful milliner.

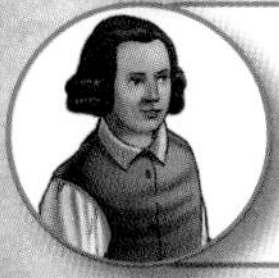

Samuel Nichols A **journeyman** of Edward Charlton. After an **apprenticeship** with another wigmaker, he took a job with Charlton. Nichols hopes to open his own wig shop one day.

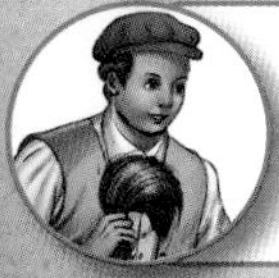

Thomas (Tommy) Wood Edward Charlton's newest apprentice. Tommy is 13, and his **contract** with Charlton is for five years.

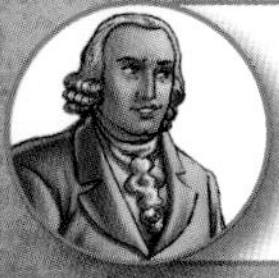

Abraham Davis A wealthy merchant. He has just moved to Williamsburg and is in need of Charlton's services.

THE LIFE OF A COLONIAL WIGMAKER

IN THE MID-1700S, EDWARD CHARLTON HAD A BUSY SHOP ON DUKE OF GLOUCESTER STREET IN WILLIAMSBURG, VIRGINIA. WEARING A WIG WAS A SIGN OF **STATUS**, AND WIGS NEEDED TO LOOK FRESH TO MAKE A GOOD IMPRESSION.

Virginia

Williamsburg

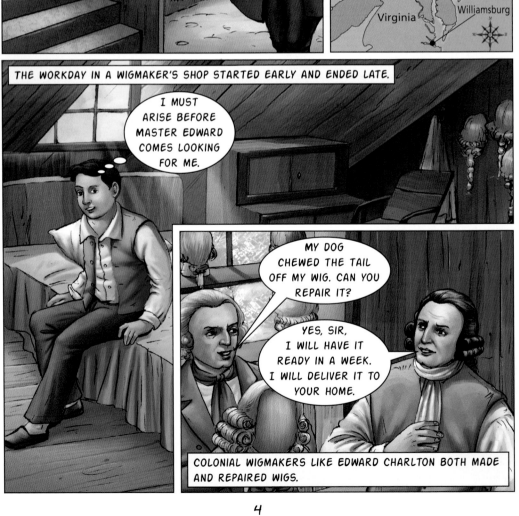

THE WORKDAY IN A WIGMAKER'S SHOP STARTED EARLY AND ENDED LATE.

I MUST ARISE BEFORE MASTER EDWARD COMES LOOKING FOR ME.

MY DOG CHEWED THE TAIL OFF MY WIG. CAN YOU REPAIR IT?

YES, SIR, I WILL HAVE IT READY IN A WEEK. I WILL DELIVER IT TO YOUR HOME.

COLONIAL WIGMAKERS LIKE EDWARD CHARLTON BOTH MADE AND REPAIRED WIGS.

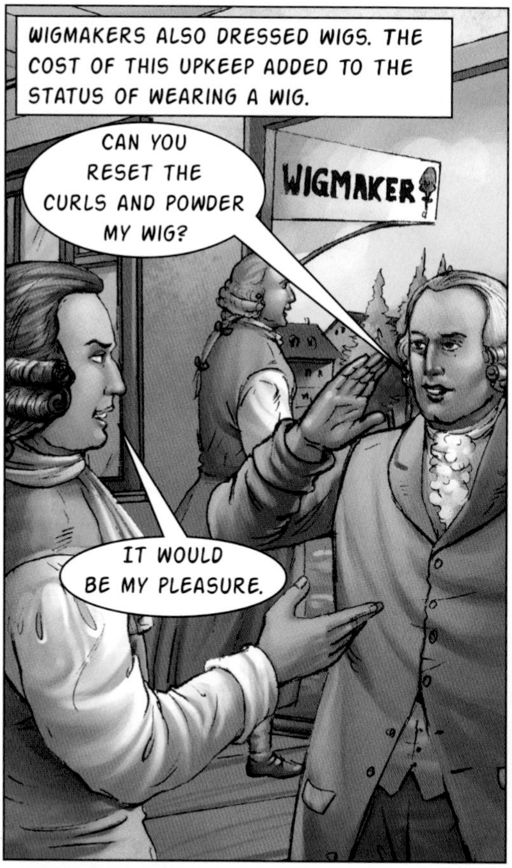
WIGMAKERS ALSO DRESSED WIGS. THE COST OF THIS UPKEEP ADDED TO THE STATUS OF WEARING A WIG.
WIGMAKER
CAN YOU RESET THE CURLS AND POWDER MY WIG?
IT WOULD BE MY PLEASURE.

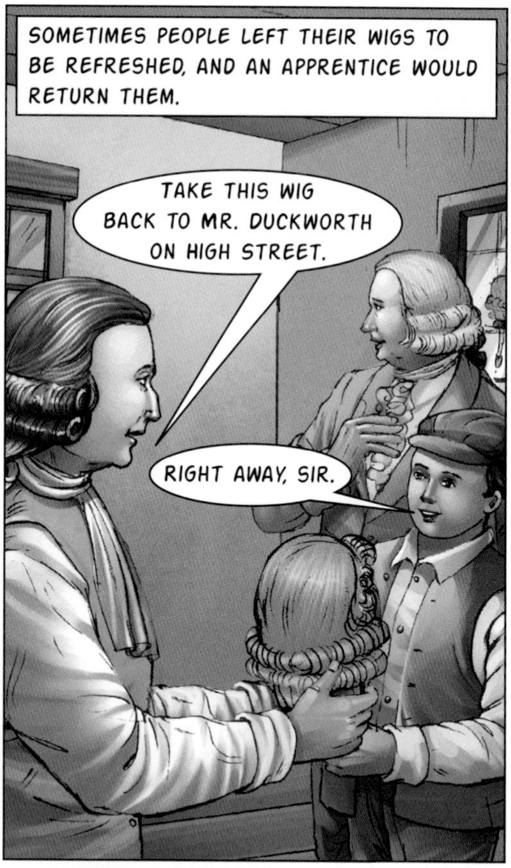
SOMETIMES PEOPLE LEFT THEIR WIGS TO BE REFRESHED, AND AN APPRENTICE WOULD RETURN THEM.
TAKE THIS WIG BACK TO MR. DUCKWORTH ON HIGH STREET.
RIGHT AWAY, SIR.

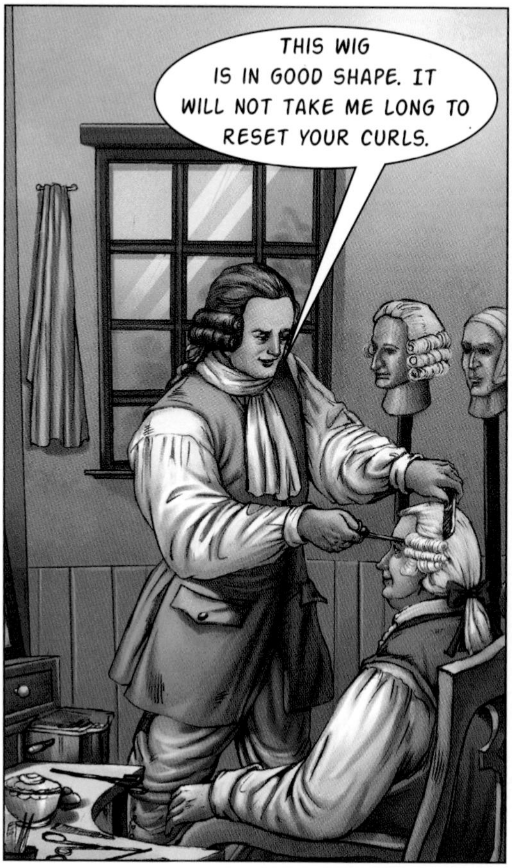
THIS WIG IS IN GOOD SHAPE. IT WILL NOT TAKE ME LONG TO RESET YOUR CURLS.

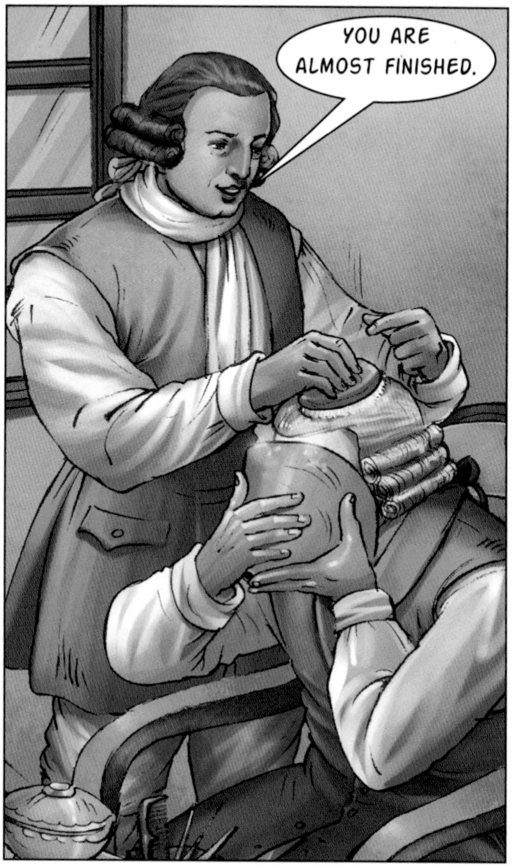
YOU ARE ALMOST FINISHED.

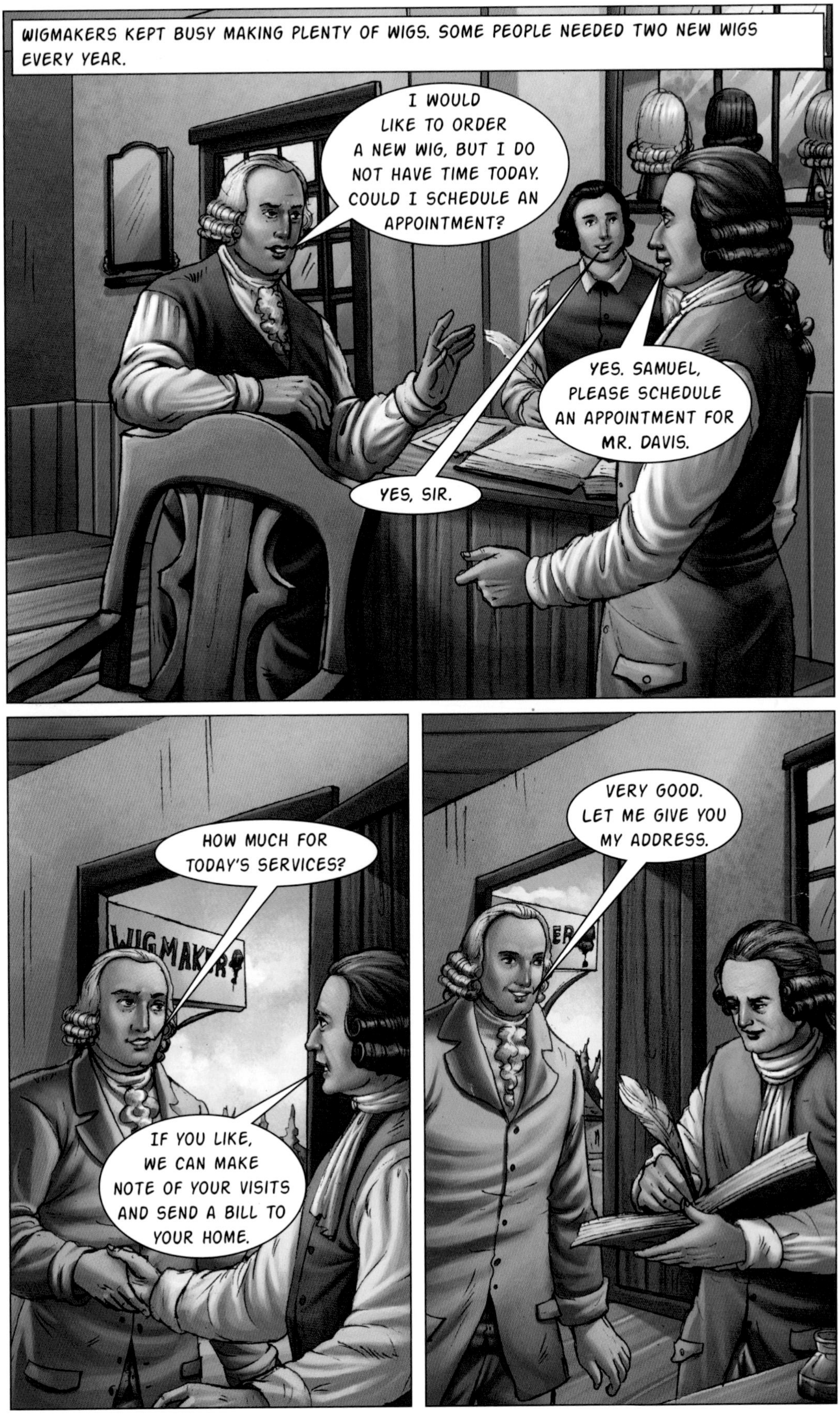
WIGMAKERS KEPT BUSY MAKING PLENTY OF WIGS. SOME PEOPLE NEEDED TWO NEW WIGS EVERY YEAR.
I WOULD LIKE TO ORDER A NEW WIG, BUT I DO NOT HAVE TIME TODAY. COULD I SCHEDULE AN APPOINTMENT?
YES. SAMUEL, PLEASE SCHEDULE AN APPOINTMENT FOR MR. DAVIS.
YES, SIR.
HOW MUCH FOR TODAY'S SERVICES?
IF YOU LIKE, WE CAN MAKE NOTE OF YOUR VISITS AND SEND A BILL TO YOUR HOME.
VERY GOOD. LET ME GIVE YOU MY ADDRESS.

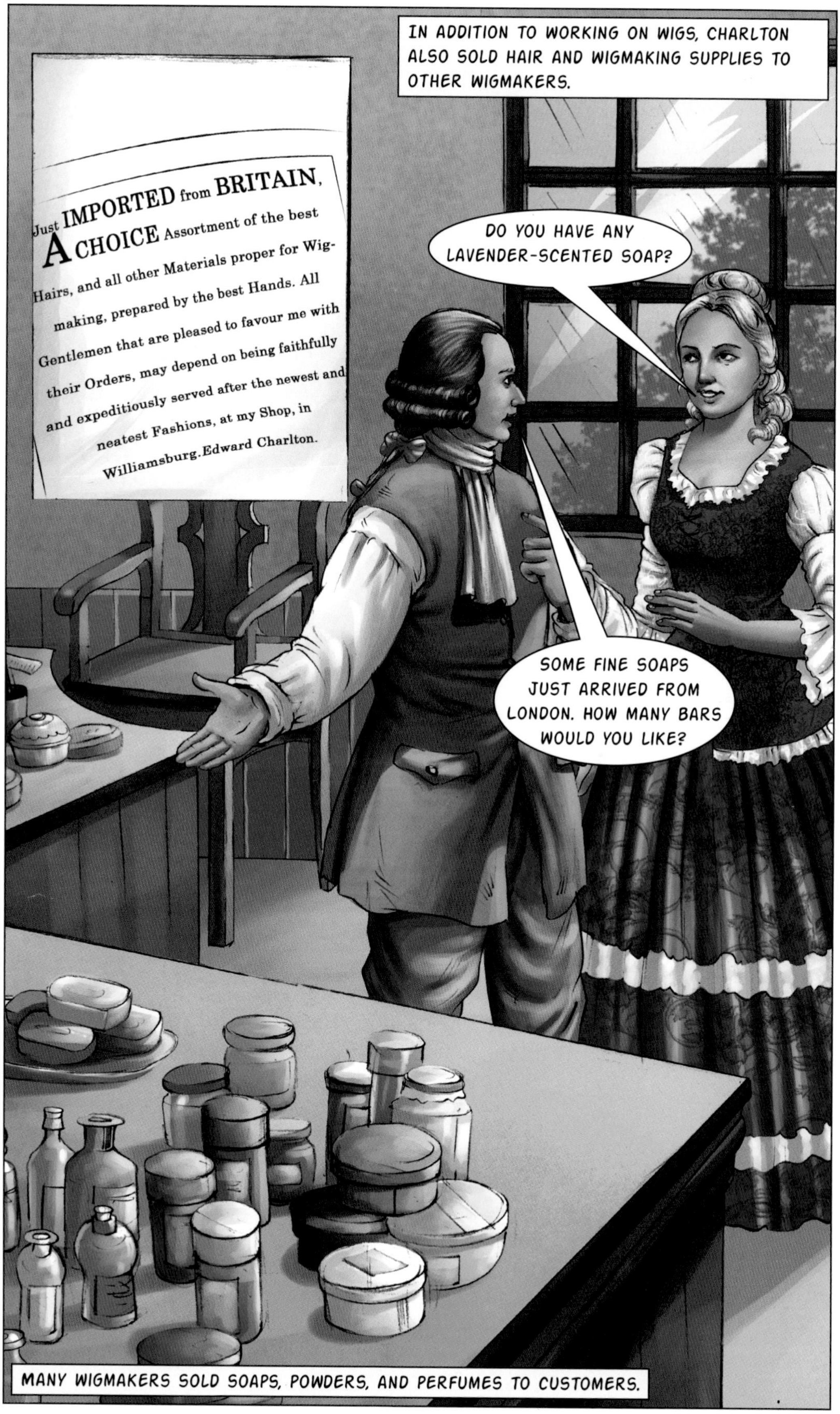
IN ADDITION TO WORKING ON WIGS, CHARLTON ALSO SOLD HAIR AND WIGMAKING SUPPLIES TO OTHER WIGMAKERS.
Just IMPORTED from BRITAIN, A CHOICE Assortment of the best Hairs, and all other Materials proper for Wig-making, prepared by the best Hands. All Gentlemen that are pleased to favour me with their Orders, may depend on being faithfully and expeditiously served after the newest and neatest Fashions, at my Shop, in Williamsburg. Edward Charlton.
DO YOU HAVE ANY LAVENDER-SCENTED SOAP?
SOME FINE SOAPS JUST ARRIVED FROM LONDON. HOW MANY BARS WOULD YOU LIKE?
MANY WIGMAKERS SOLD SOAPS, POWDERS, AND PERFUMES TO CUSTOMERS.

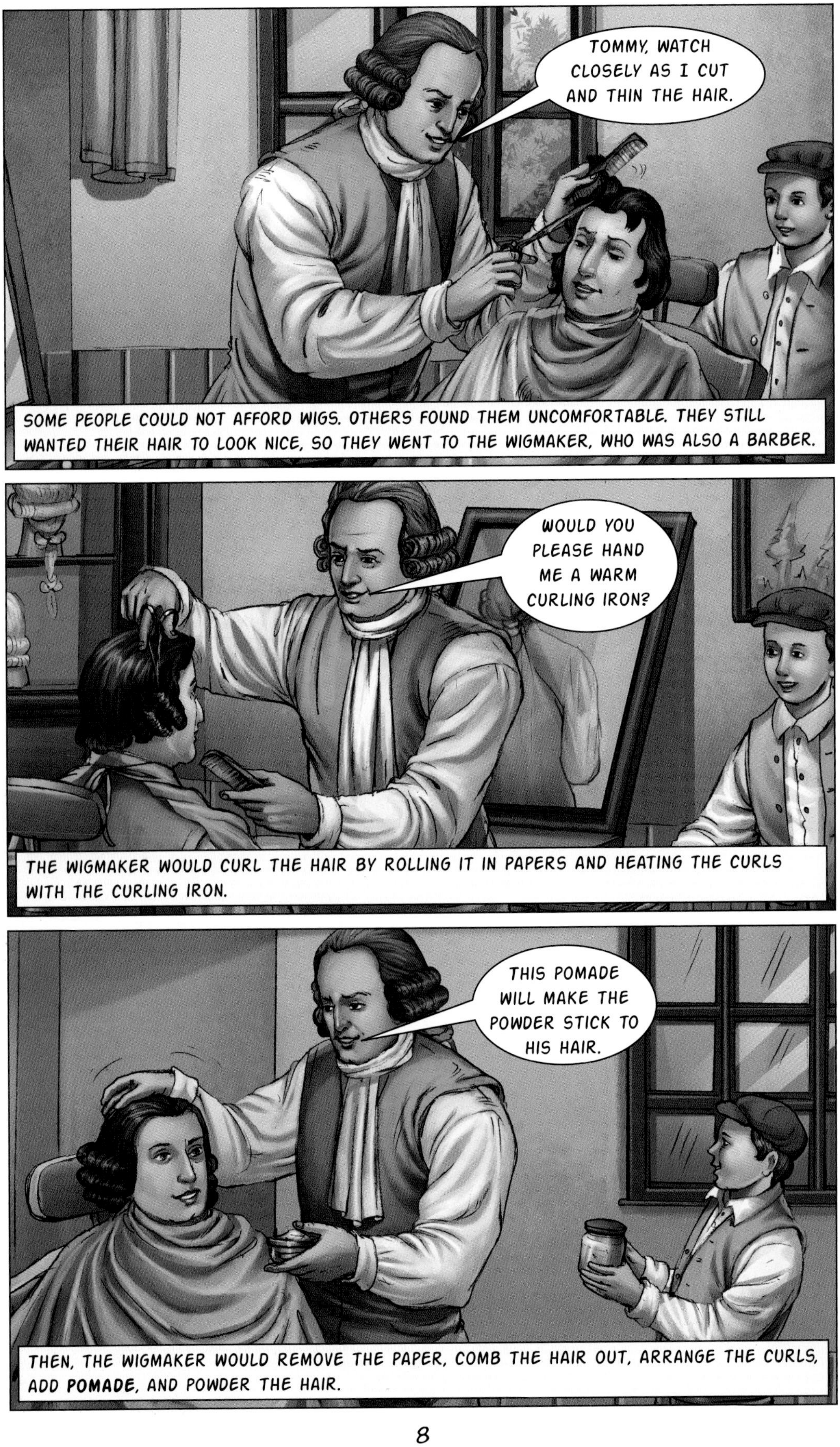
TOMMY, WATCH CLOSELY AS I CUT AND THIN THE HAIR.
SOME PEOPLE COULD NOT AFFORD WIGS. OTHERS FOUND THEM UNCOMFORTABLE. THEY STILL WANTED THEIR HAIR TO LOOK NICE, SO THEY WENT TO THE WIGMAKER, WHO WAS ALSO A BARBER.
WOULD YOU PLEASE HAND ME A WARM CURLING IRON?
THE WIGMAKER WOULD CURL THE HAIR BY ROLLING IT IN PAPERS AND HEATING THE CURLS WITH THE CURLING IRON.
THIS POMADE WILL MAKE THE POWDER STICK TO HIS HAIR.
THEN, THE WIGMAKER WOULD REMOVE THE PAPER, COMB THE HAIR OUT, ARRANGE THE CURLS, ADD **POMADE**, AND POWDER THE HAIR.

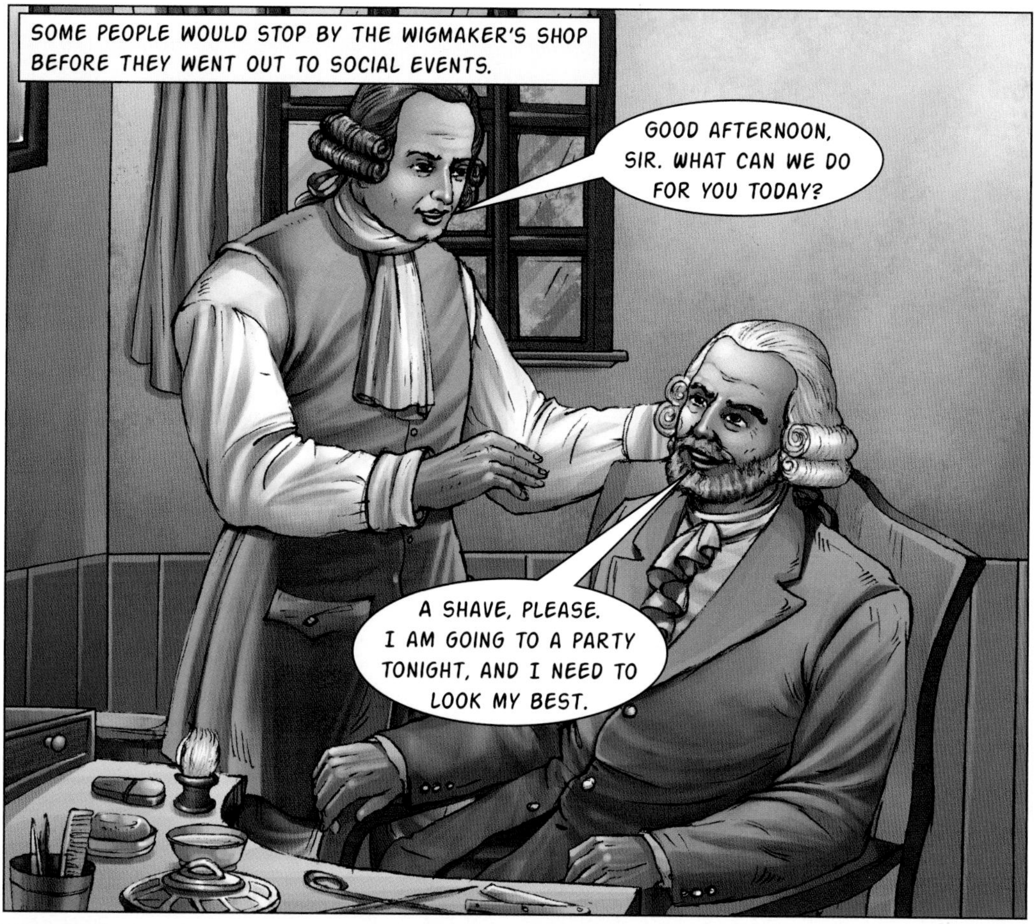
SOME PEOPLE WOULD STOP BY THE WIGMAKER'S SHOP BEFORE THEY WENT OUT TO SOCIAL EVENTS.
GOOD AFTERNOON, SIR. WHAT CAN WE DO FOR YOU TODAY?
A SHAVE, PLEASE. I AM GOING TO A PARTY TONIGHT, AND I NEED TO LOOK MY BEST.

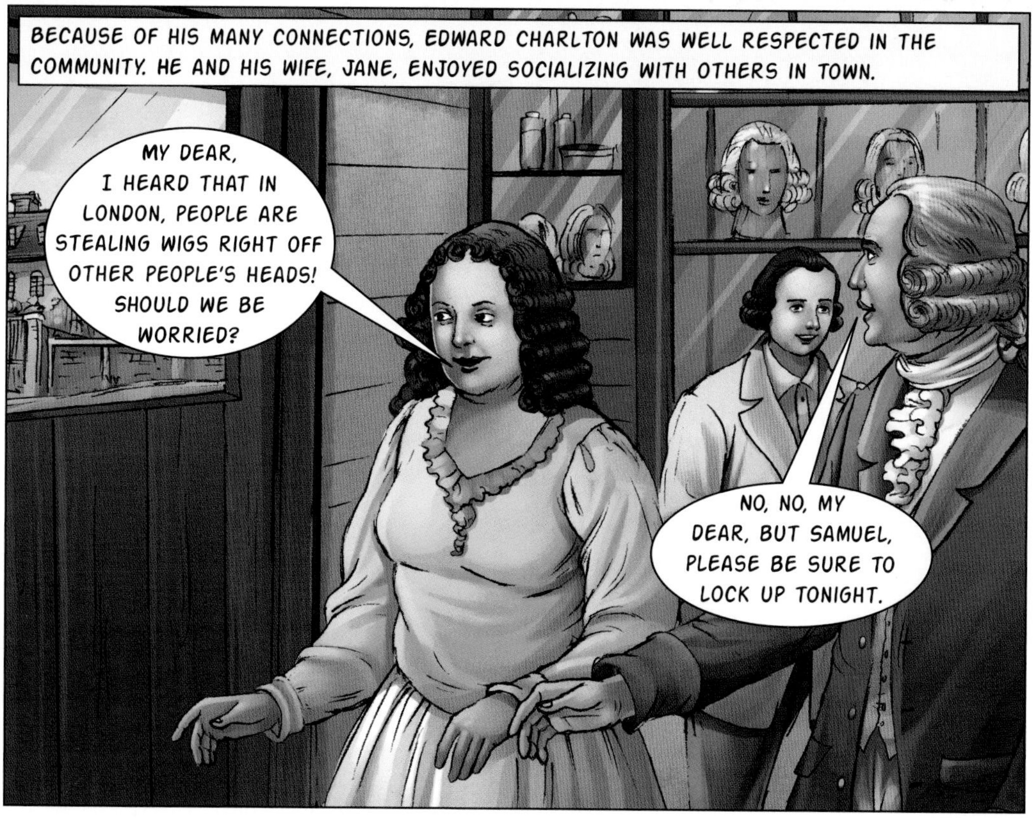
BECAUSE OF HIS MANY CONNECTIONS, EDWARD CHARLTON WAS WELL RESPECTED IN THE COMMUNITY. HE AND HIS WIFE, JANE, ENJOYED SOCIALIZING WITH OTHERS IN TOWN.
MY DEAR, I HEARD THAT IN LONDON, PEOPLE ARE STEALING WIGS RIGHT OFF OTHER PEOPLE'S HEADS! SHOULD WE BE WORRIED?
NO, NO, MY DEAR, BUT SAMUEL, PLEASE BE SURE TO LOCK UP TONIGHT.

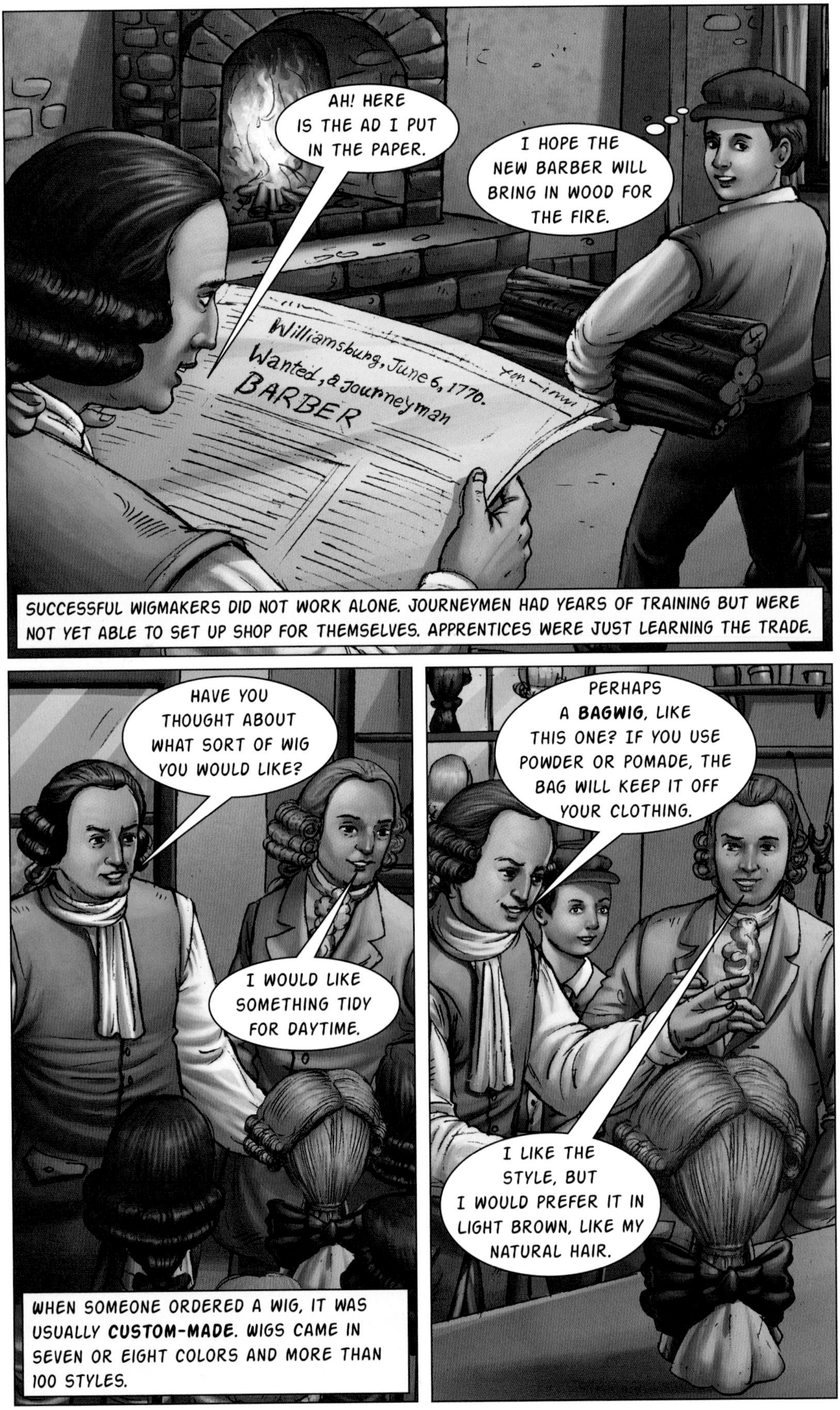
AH! HERE IS THE AD I PUT IN THE PAPER.
Williamsburg, June 6, 1770.
Wanted, a Journeyman
BARBER
I HOPE THE NEW BARBER WILL BRING IN WOOD FOR THE FIRE.
SUCCESSFUL WIGMAKERS DID NOT WORK ALONE. JOURNEYMEN HAD YEARS OF TRAINING BUT WERE NOT YET ABLE TO SET UP SHOP FOR THEMSELVES. APPRENTICES WERE JUST LEARNING THE TRADE.
HAVE YOU THOUGHT ABOUT WHAT SORT OF WIG YOU WOULD LIKE?
I WOULD LIKE SOMETHING TIDY FOR DAYTIME.
WHEN SOMEONE ORDERED A WIG, IT WAS USUALLY **CUSTOM-MADE**. WIGS CAME IN SEVEN OR EIGHT COLORS AND MORE THAN 100 STYLES.
PERHAPS A **BAGWIG**, LIKE THIS ONE? IF YOU USE POWDER OR POMADE, THE BAG WILL KEEP IT OFF YOUR CLOTHING.
I LIKE THE STYLE, BUT I WOULD PREFER IT IN LIGHT BROWN, LIKE MY NATURAL HAIR.

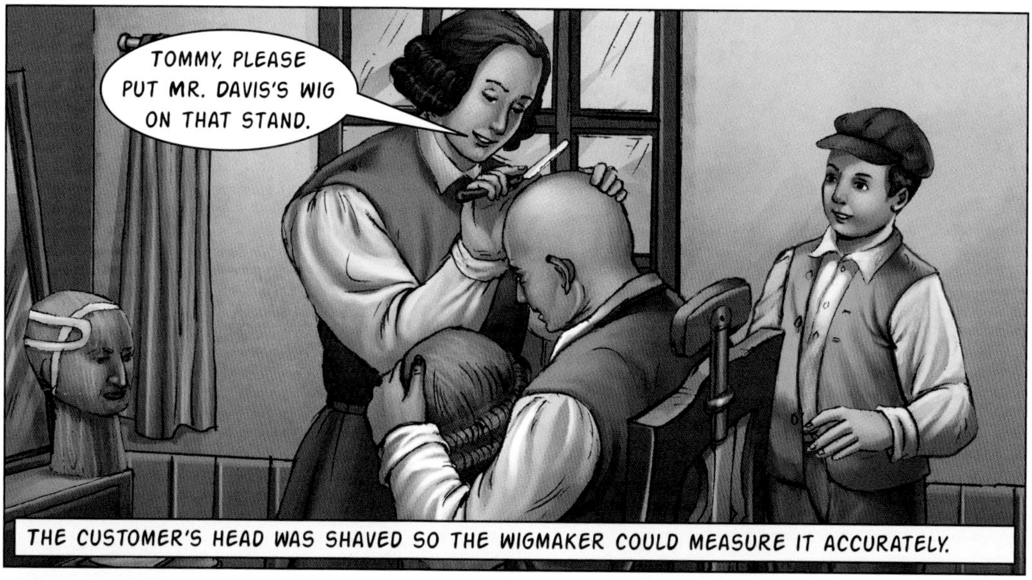
TOMMY, PLEASE PUT MR. DAVIS'S WIG ON THAT STAND.
THE CUSTOMER'S HEAD WAS SHAVED SO THE WIGMAKER COULD MEASURE IT ACCURATELY.

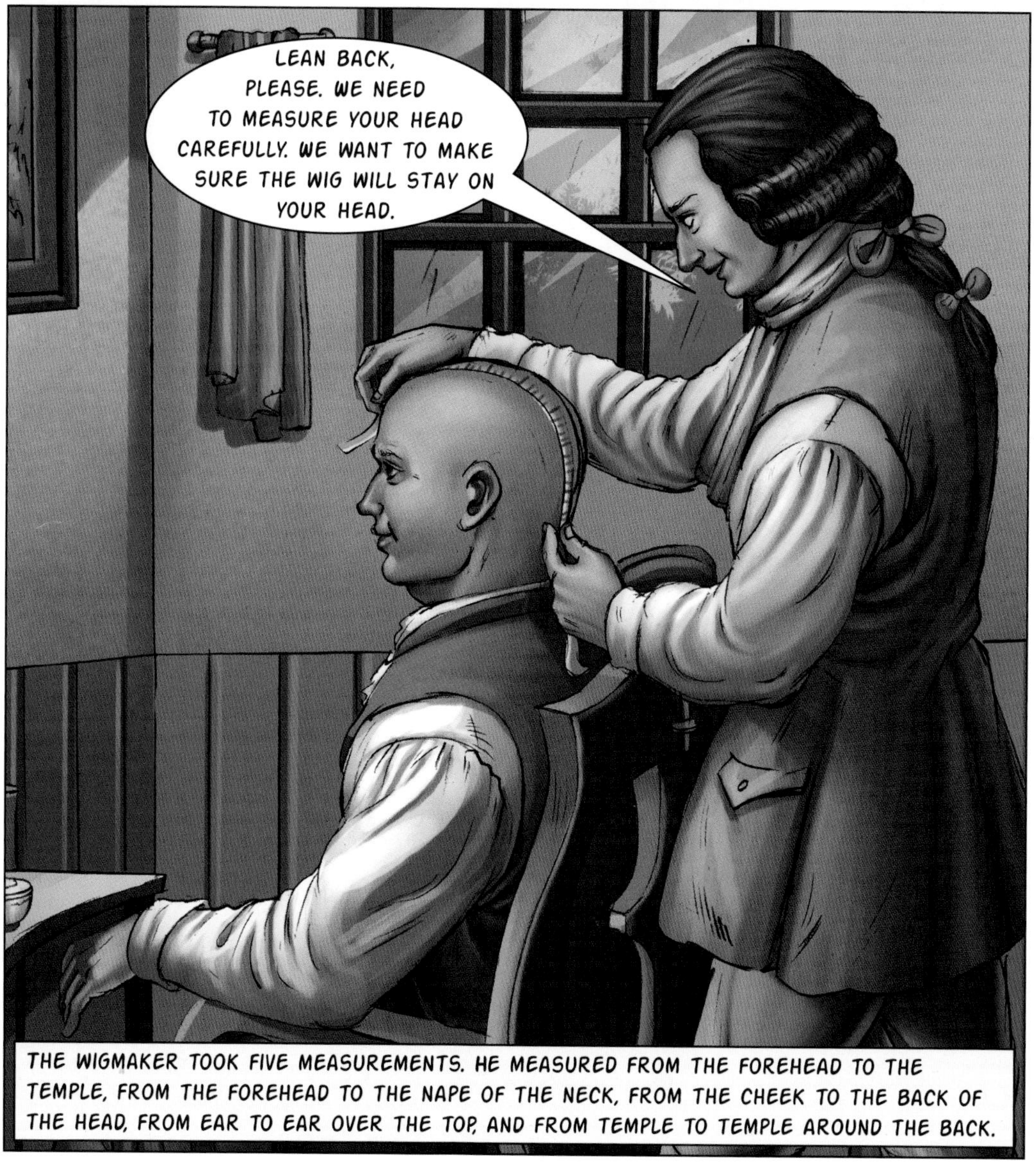
LEAN BACK, PLEASE. WE NEED TO MEASURE YOUR HEAD CAREFULLY. WE WANT TO MAKE SURE THE WIG WILL STAY ON YOUR HEAD.
THE WIGMAKER TOOK FIVE MEASUREMENTS. HE MEASURED FROM THE FOREHEAD TO THE TEMPLE, FROM THE FOREHEAD TO THE NAPE OF THE NECK, FROM THE CHEEK TO THE BACK OF THE HEAD, FROM EAR TO EAR OVER THE TOP, AND FROM TEMPLE TO TEMPLE AROUND THE BACK.

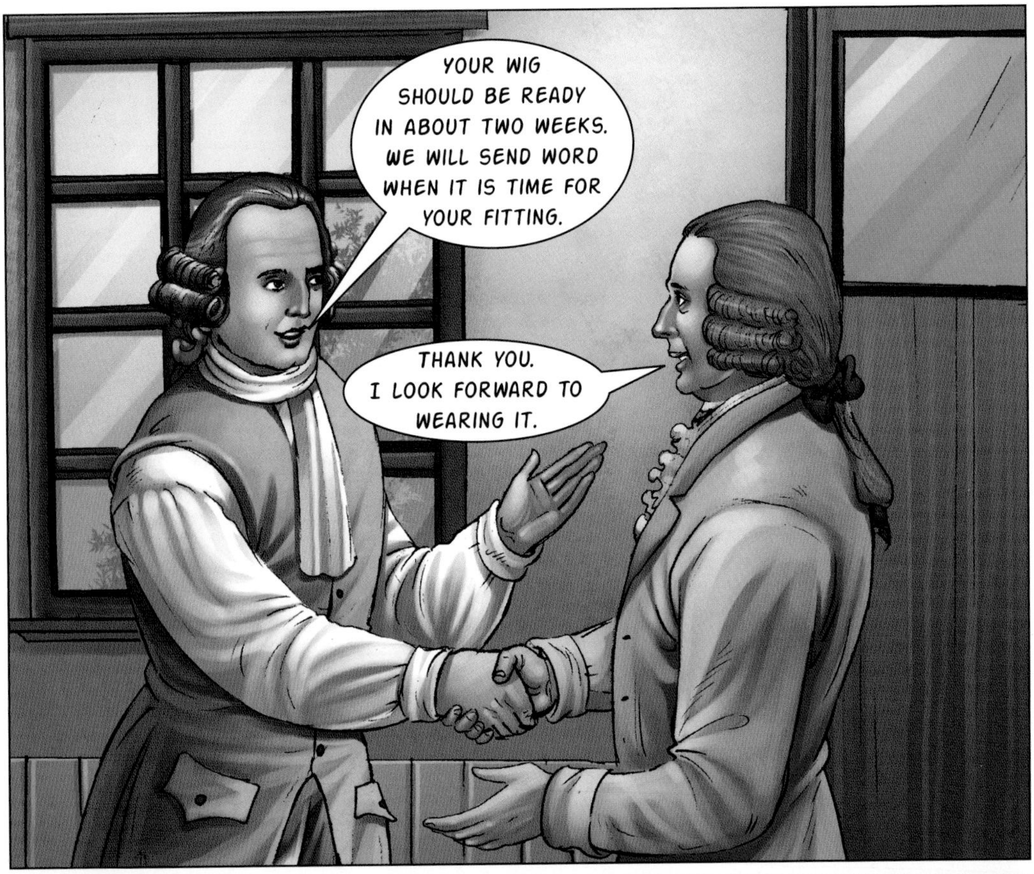
YOUR WIG SHOULD BE READY IN ABOUT TWO WEEKS. WE WILL SEND WORD WHEN IT IS TIME FOR YOUR FITTING.
THANK YOU. I LOOK FORWARD TO WEARING IT.

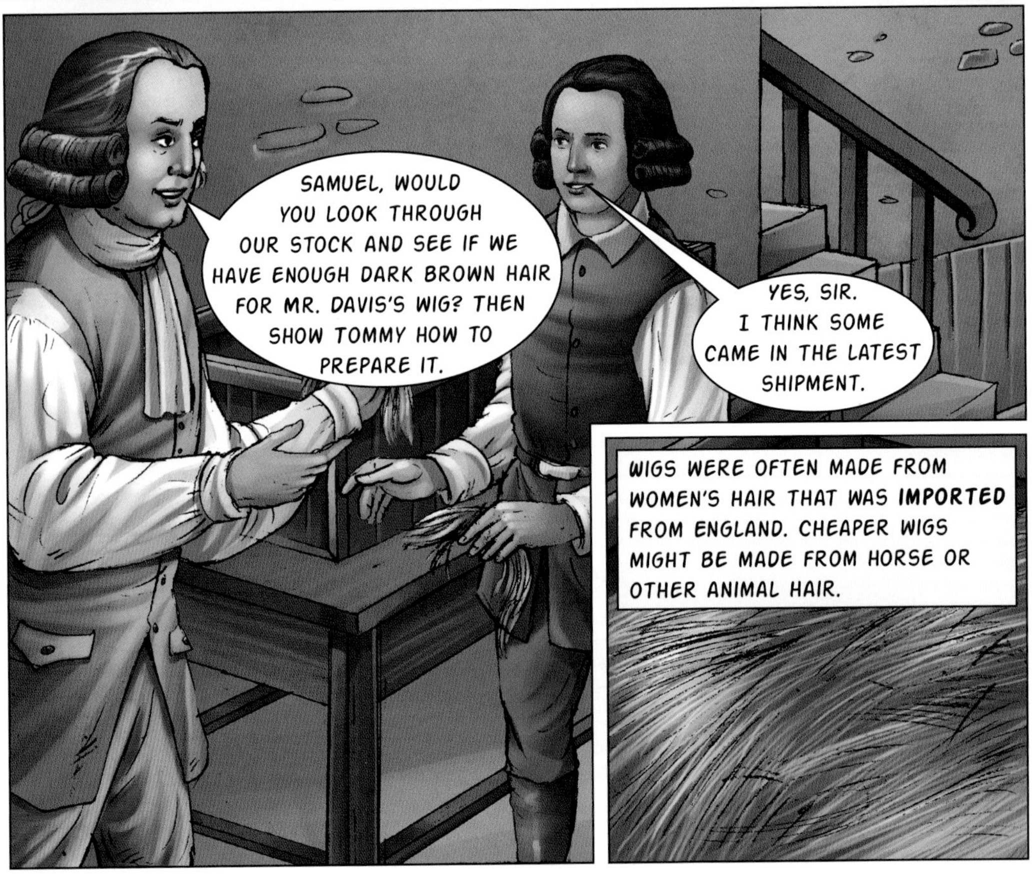
SAMUEL, WOULD YOU LOOK THROUGH OUR STOCK AND SEE IF WE HAVE ENOUGH DARK BROWN HAIR FOR MR. DAVIS'S WIG? THEN SHOW TOMMY HOW TO PREPARE IT.
YES, SIR. I THINK SOME CAME IN THE LATEST SHIPMENT.
WIGS WERE OFTEN MADE FROM WOMEN'S HAIR THAT WAS **IMPORTED** FROM ENGLAND. CHEAPER WIGS MIGHT BE MADE FROM HORSE OR OTHER ANIMAL HAIR.

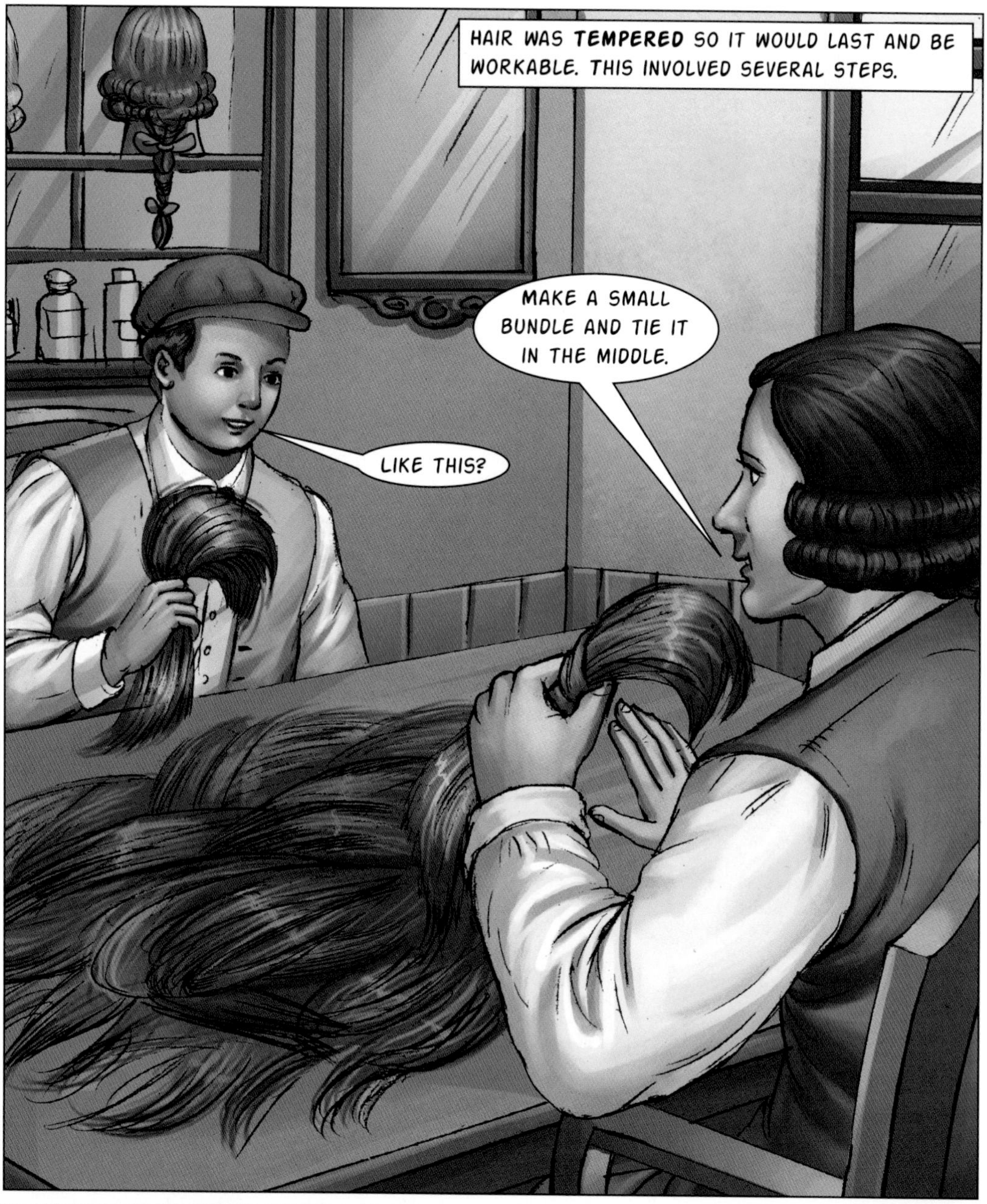
HAIR WAS **TEMPERED** SO IT WOULD LAST AND BE WORKABLE. THIS INVOLVED SEVERAL STEPS.
MAKE A SMALL BUNDLE AND TIE IT IN THE MIDDLE.
LIKE THIS?

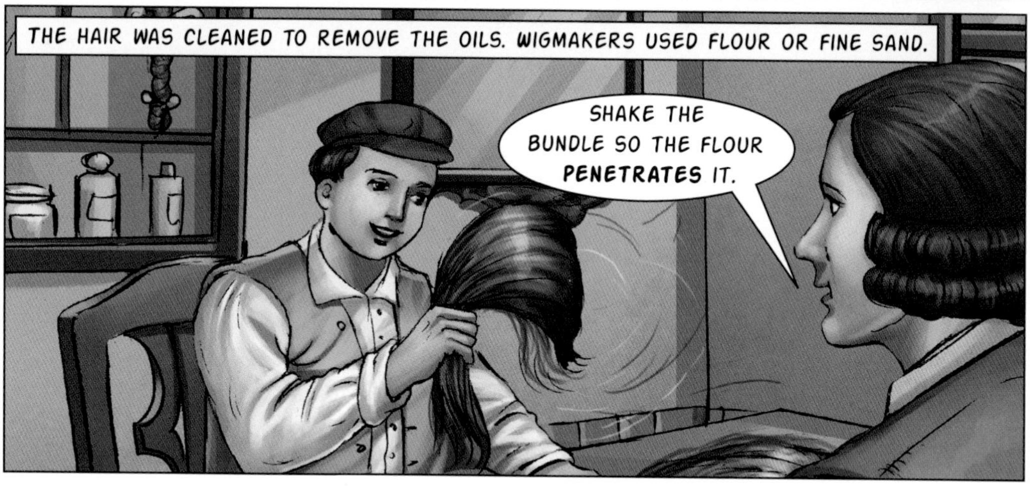
THE HAIR WAS CLEANED TO REMOVE THE OILS. WIGMAKERS USED FLOUR OR FINE SAND.
SHAKE THE BUNDLE SO THE FLOUR **PENETRATES** IT.

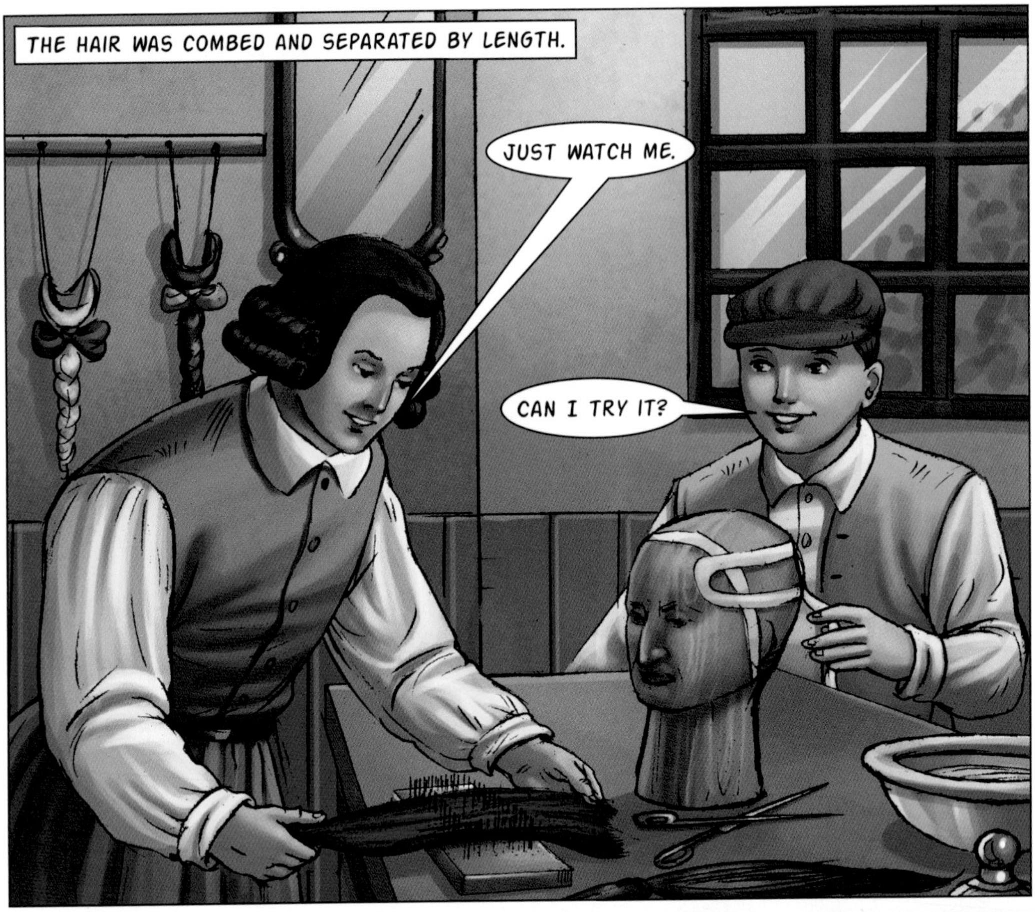
THE HAIR WAS COMBED AND SEPARATED BY LENGTH.
JUST WATCH ME.
CAN I TRY IT?

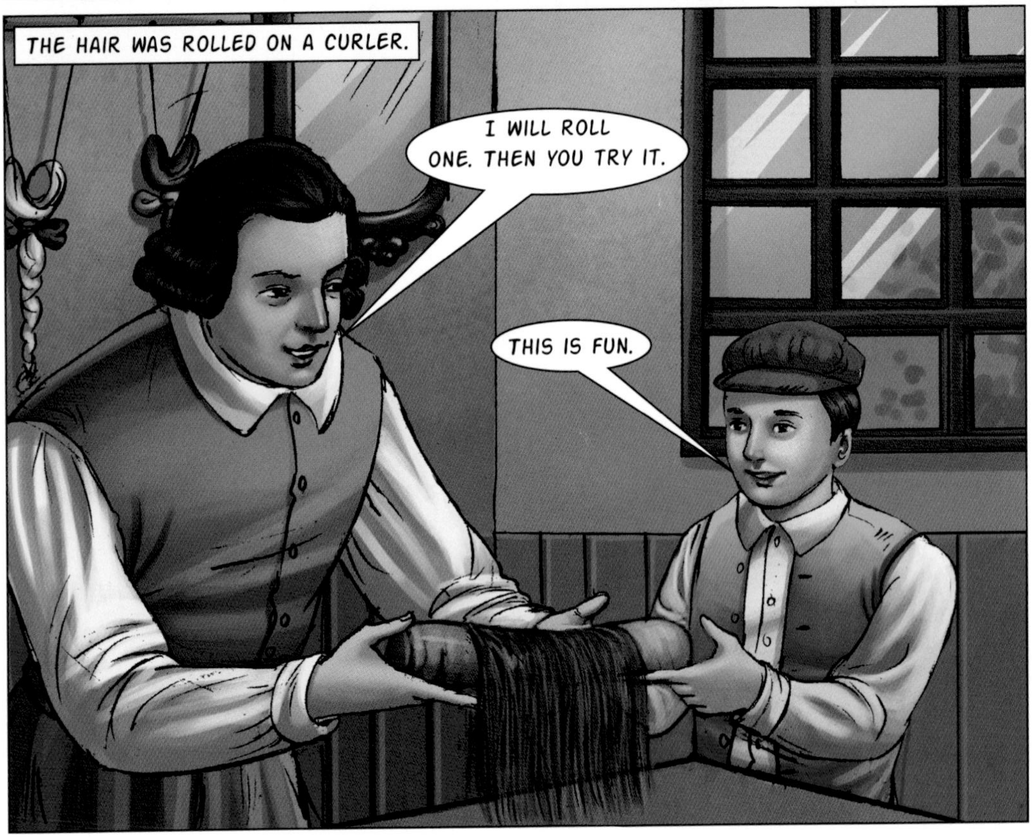
THE HAIR WAS ROLLED ON A CURLER.
I WILL ROLL ONE. THEN YOU TRY IT.
THIS IS FUN.

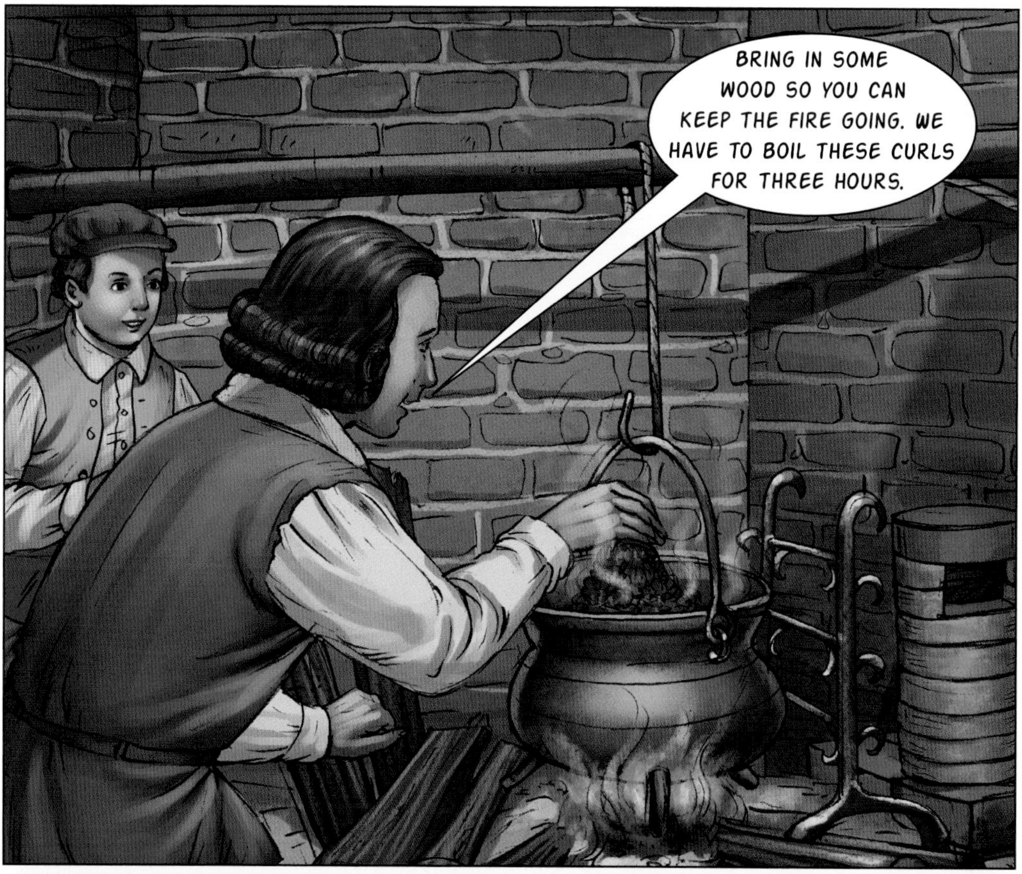
BRING IN SOME WOOD SO YOU CAN KEEP THE FIRE GOING. WE HAVE TO BOIL THESE CURLS FOR THREE HOURS.

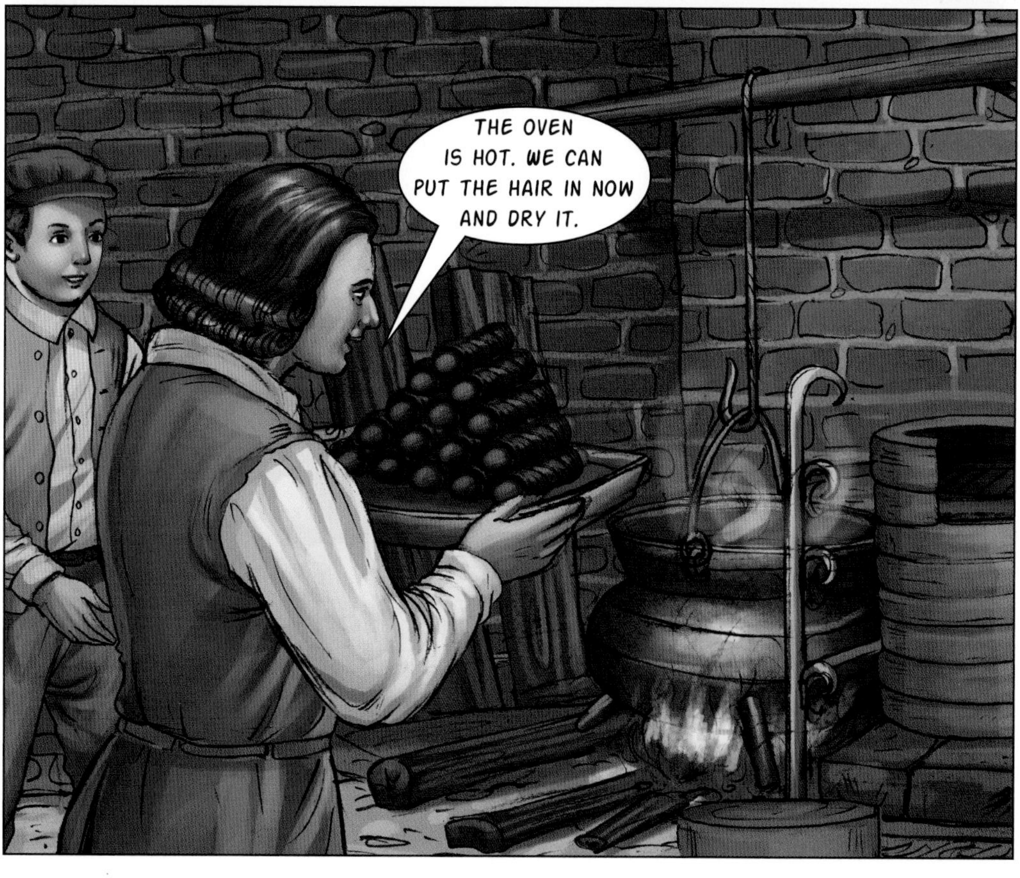
THE OVEN IS HOT. WE CAN PUT THE HAIR IN NOW AND DRY IT.

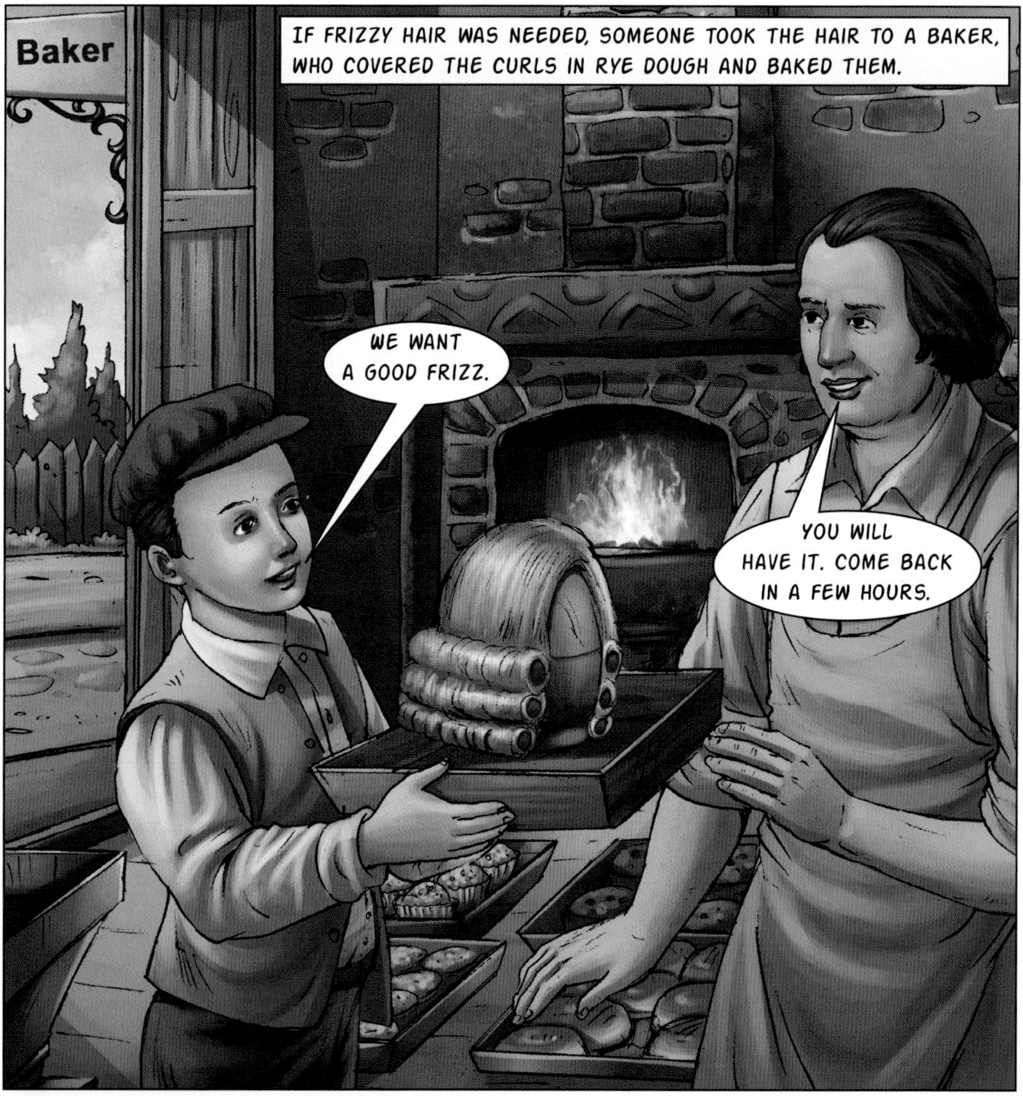
Baker
IF FRIZZY HAIR WAS NEEDED, SOMEONE TOOK THE HAIR TO A BAKER, WHO COVERED THE CURLS IN RYE DOUGH AND BAKED THEM.
WE WANT A GOOD FRIZZ.
YOU WILL HAVE IT. COME BACK IN A FEW HOURS.

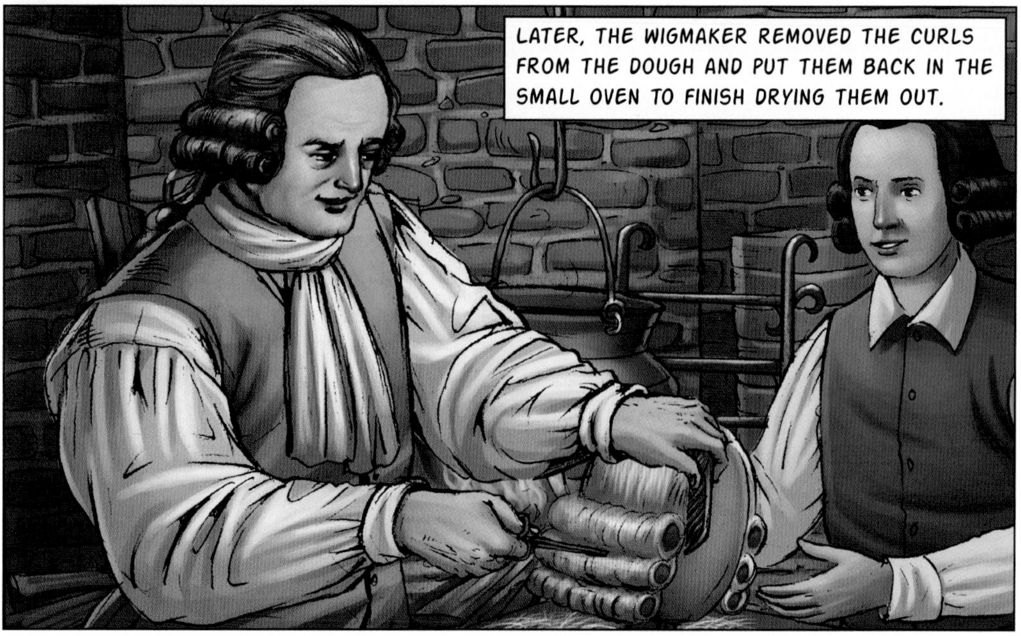
LATER, THE WIGMAKER REMOVED THE CURLS FROM THE DOUGH AND PUT THEM BACK IN THE SMALL OVEN TO FINISH DRYING THEM OUT.

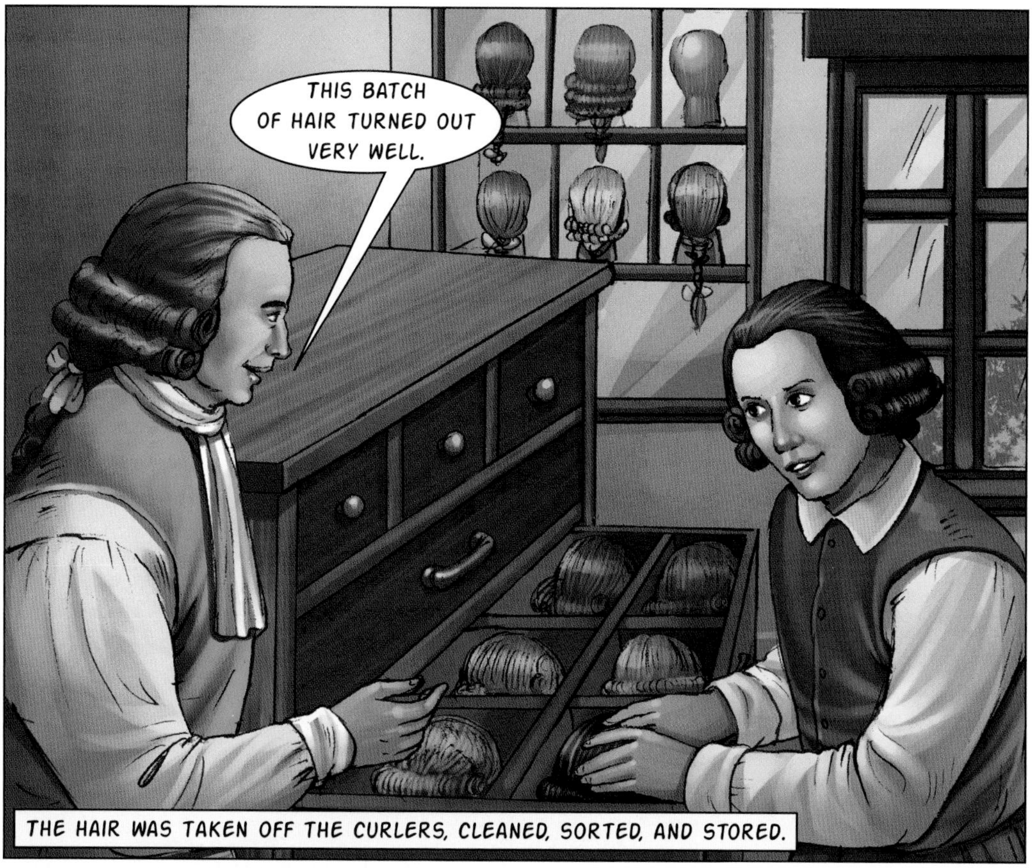
THIS BATCH OF HAIR TURNED OUT VERY WELL.
THE HAIR WAS TAKEN OFF THE CURLERS, CLEANED, SORTED, AND STORED.

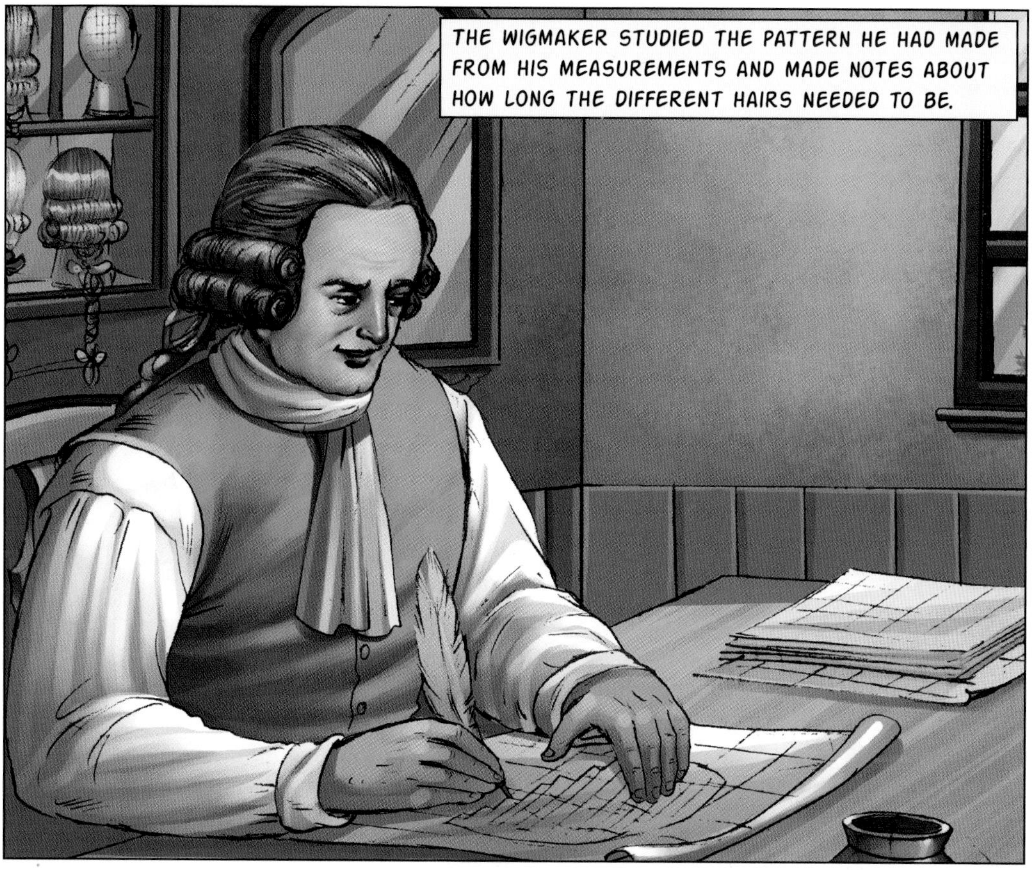
THE WIGMAKER STUDIED THE PATTERN HE HAD MADE FROM HIS MEASUREMENTS AND MADE NOTES ABOUT HOW LONG THE DIFFERENT HAIRS NEEDED TO BE.

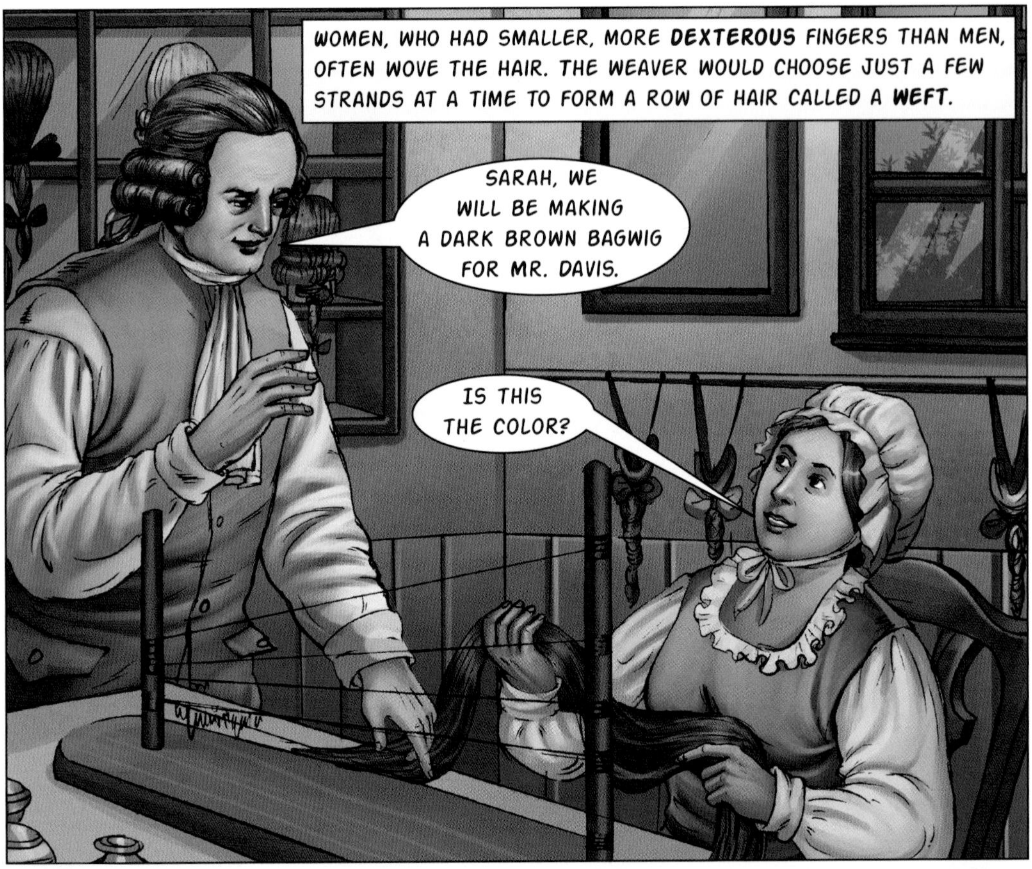
WOMEN, WHO HAD SMALLER, MORE **DEXTEROUS** FINGERS THAN MEN, OFTEN WOVE THE HAIR. THE WEAVER WOULD CHOOSE JUST A FEW STRANDS AT A TIME TO FORM A ROW OF HAIR CALLED A **WEFT**.
SARAH, WE WILL BE MAKING A DARK BROWN BAGWIG FOR MR. DAVIS.
IS THIS THE COLOR?

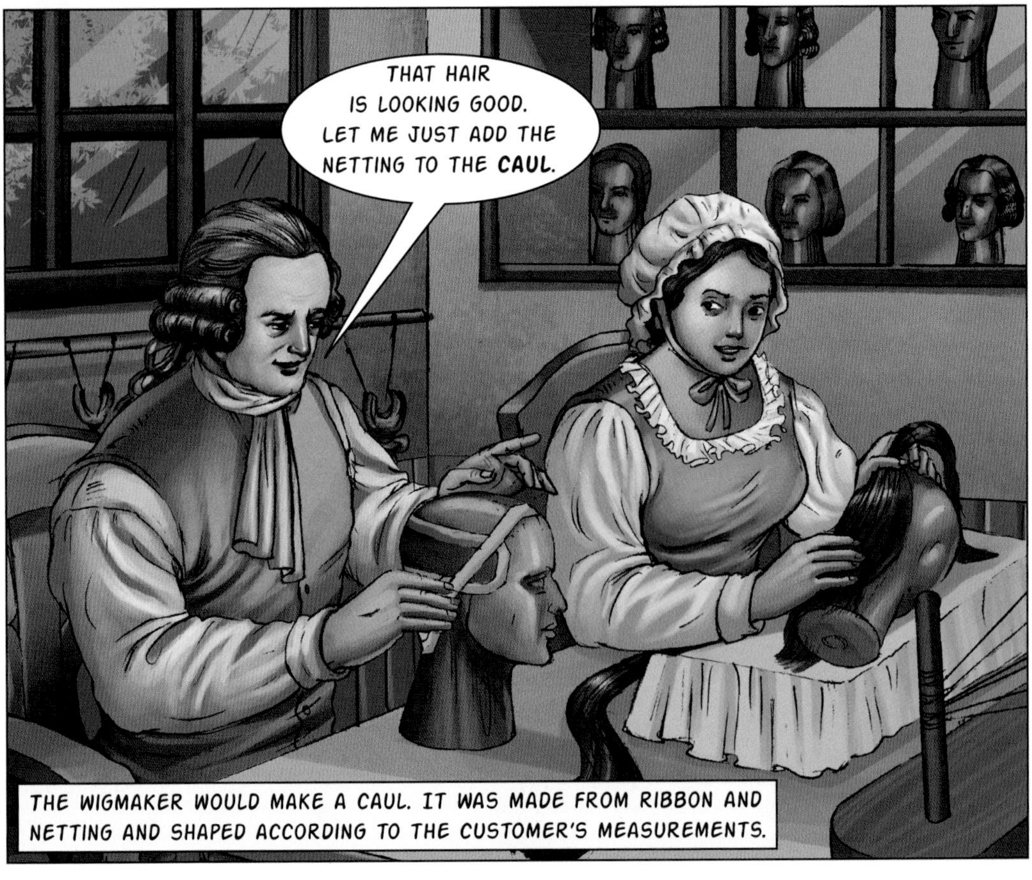
THAT HAIR IS LOOKING GOOD. LET ME JUST ADD THE NETTING TO THE **CAUL**.
THE WIGMAKER WOULD MAKE A CAUL. IT WAS MADE FROM RIBBON AND NETTING AND SHAPED ACCORDING TO THE CUSTOMER'S MEASUREMENTS.

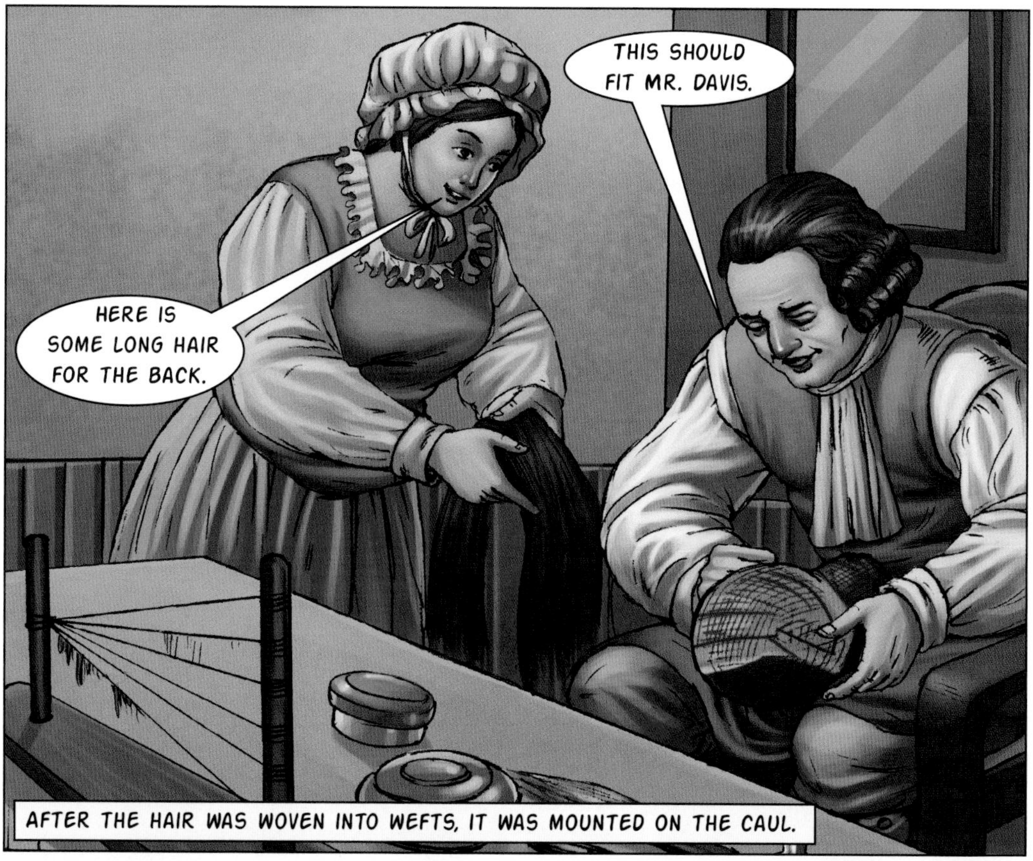
THIS SHOULD FIT MR. DAVIS.
HERE IS SOME LONG HAIR FOR THE BACK.
AFTER THE HAIR WAS WOVEN INTO WEFTS, IT WAS MOUNTED ON THE CAUL.

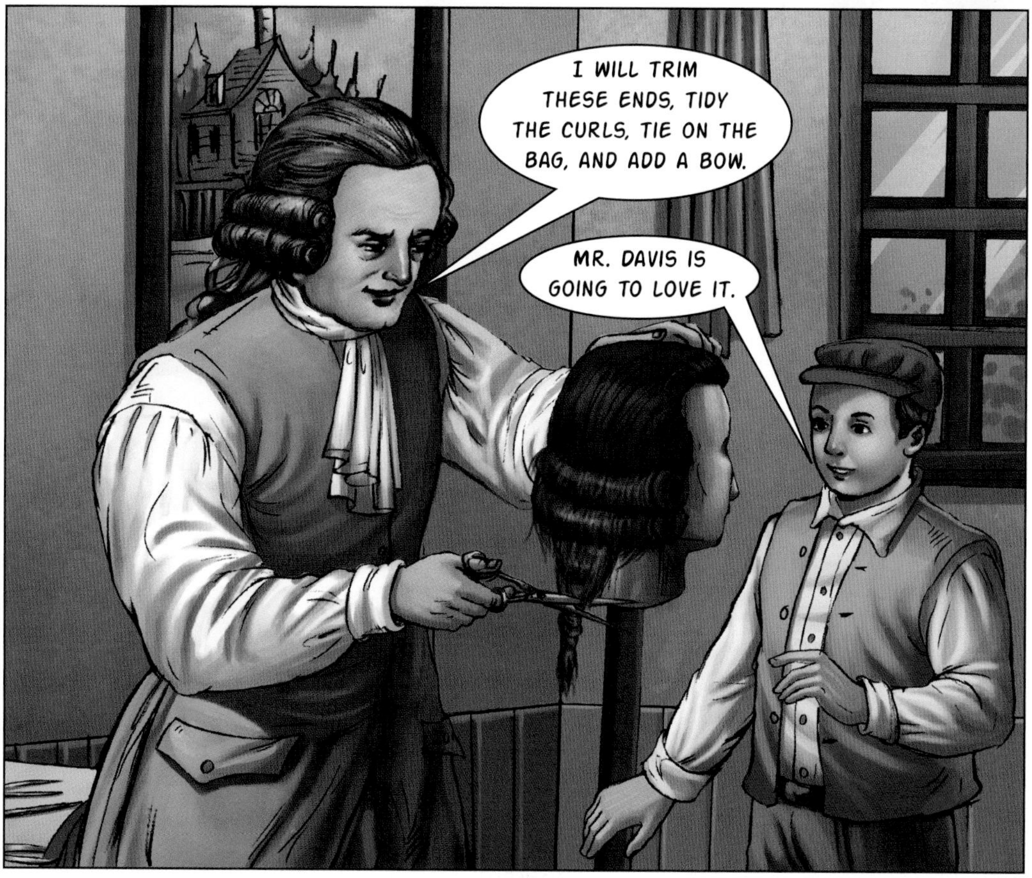
I WILL TRIM THESE ENDS, TIDY THE CURLS, TIE ON THE BAG, AND ADD A BOW.
MR. DAVIS IS GOING TO LOVE IT.

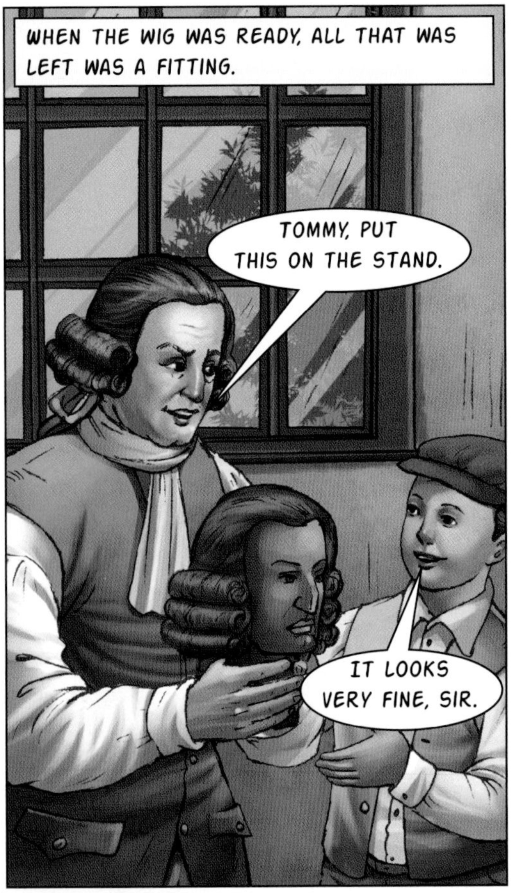
WHEN THE WIG WAS READY, ALL THAT WAS LEFT WAS A FITTING.
TOMMY, PUT THIS ON THE STAND.
IT LOOKS VERY FINE, SIR.

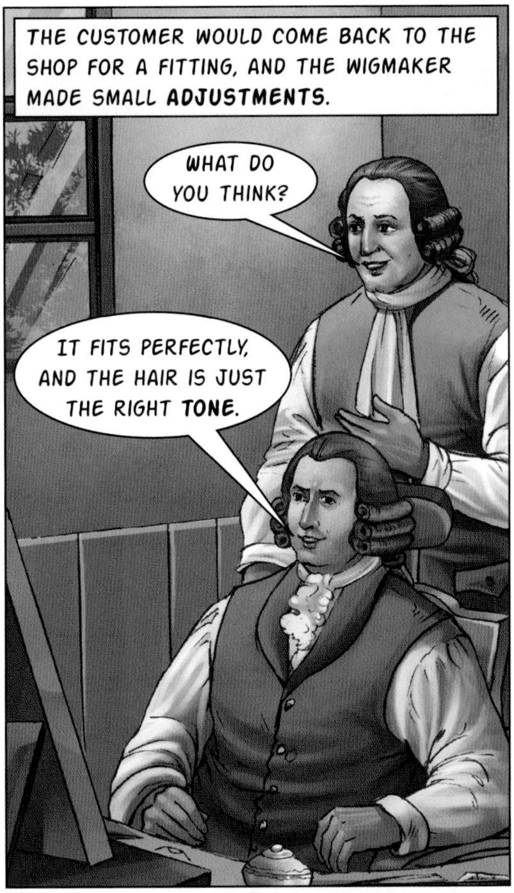
THE CUSTOMER WOULD COME BACK TO THE SHOP FOR A FITTING, AND THE WIGMAKER MADE SMALL **ADJUSTMENTS**.
WHAT DO YOU THINK?
IT FITS PERFECTLY, AND THE HAIR IS JUST THE RIGHT **TONE**.

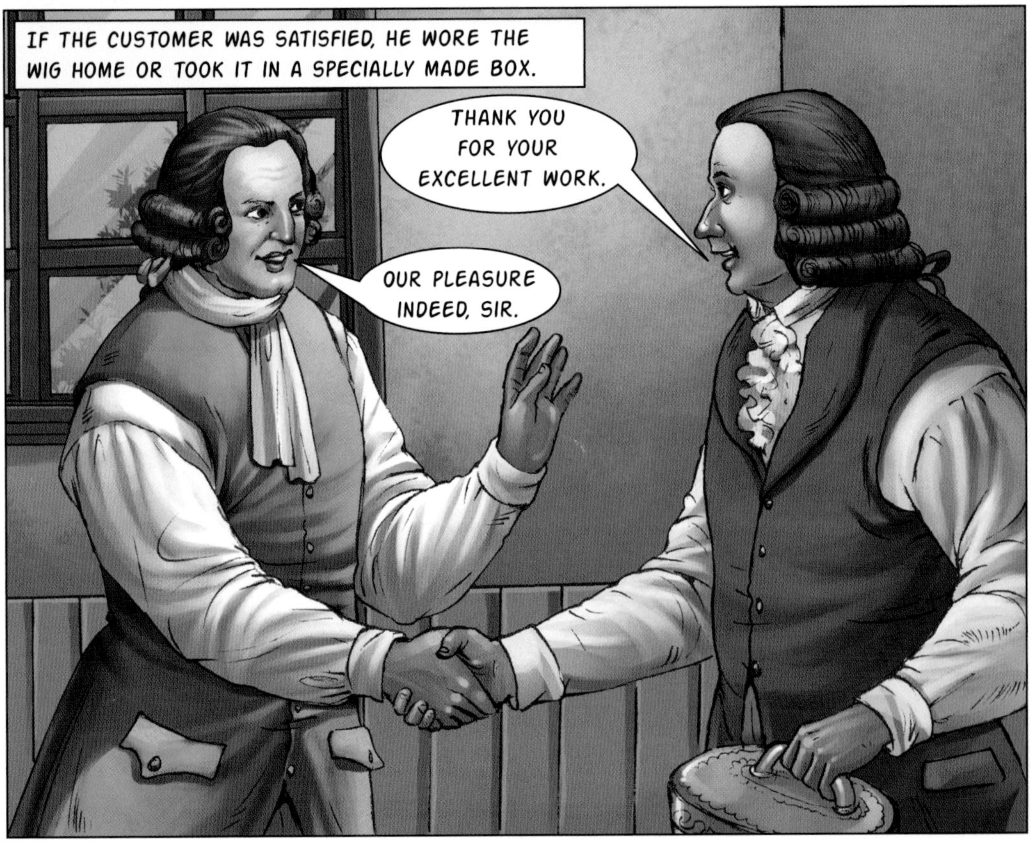
IF THE CUSTOMER WAS SATISFIED, HE WORE THE WIG HOME OR TOOK IT IN A SPECIALLY MADE BOX.
THANK YOU FOR YOUR EXCELLENT WORK.
OUR PLEASURE INDEED, SIR.

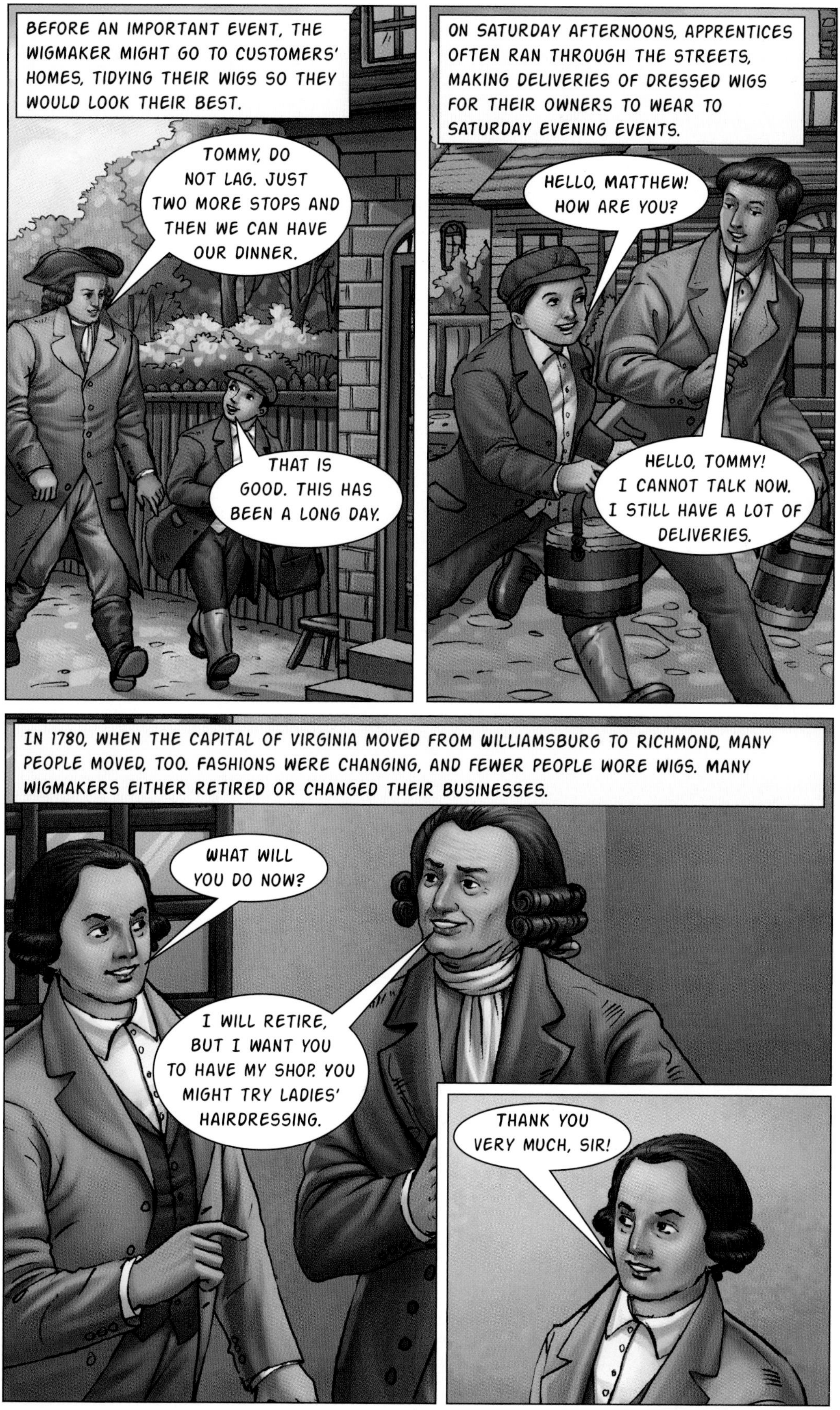
BEFORE AN IMPORTANT EVENT, THE WIGMAKER MIGHT GO TO CUSTOMERS' HOMES, TIDYING THEIR WIGS SO THEY WOULD LOOK THEIR BEST.
TOMMY, DO NOT LAG. JUST TWO MORE STOPS AND THEN WE CAN HAVE OUR DINNER.
THAT IS GOOD. THIS HAS BEEN A LONG DAY.
ON SATURDAY AFTERNOONS, APPRENTICES OFTEN RAN THROUGH THE STREETS, MAKING DELIVERIES OF DRESSED WIGS FOR THEIR OWNERS TO WEAR TO SATURDAY EVENING EVENTS.
HELLO, MATTHEW! HOW ARE YOU?
HELLO, TOMMY! I CANNOT TALK NOW. I STILL HAVE A LOT OF DELIVERIES.
IN 1780, WHEN THE CAPITAL OF VIRGINIA MOVED FROM WILLIAMSBURG TO RICHMOND, MANY PEOPLE MOVED, TOO. FASHIONS WERE CHANGING, AND FEWER PEOPLE WORE WIGS. MANY WIGMAKERS EITHER RETIRED OR CHANGED THEIR BUSINESSES.
WHAT WILL YOU DO NOW?
I WILL RETIRE, BUT I WANT YOU TO HAVE MY SHOP. YOU MIGHT TRY LADIES' HAIRDRESSING.
THANK YOU VERY MUCH, SIR!

FAMOUS COLONIAL WIGMAKERS

Alexander Finnie
(unknown–1769)

Another successful Williamsburg wigmaker active in the middle of the eighteenth century, Alexander Finnie also owned the Raleigh Tavern. The tavern was a gathering place for important people in town. Finnie's wigmaking business did well. He advertised for help, and a fellow wigmaker claimed that Finnie convinced one of his workers to leave him and work for Finnie instead.

Oliver Galtery
(unknown)

Oliver Galtery had a wigmaking shop on High Street, now Market Street, in the center of Philadelphia. He was busy enough to place an advertisement looking for light-colored hair in *The American Weekly Mercury*, the first newspaper published in the middle colonies. Galtery seems to have been generous as well. In 1722, he offered an exhibition of "the Czar of Muscovia's country seat, with its gardens, walks, fountains, fish ponds, and fish that swim" at his home.

John Piemont
(c. 1717–1802)

Born in France, John Piemont traveled to Boston and became a wigmaker around 1759. He opened a store on busy King's Street, now State Street, in Boston, and he made wigs for leading Bostonians. In 1773, he gave up wig making, possibly because his zeal for the cause of independence lost him business. He moved to Danvers, a town north of Boston, where he ran a tavern called the Turk's Head.

GLOSSARY

adjustments (uh-JUST-ments) Changes so something is in a better position.

apprenticeship (uh-PREN-tis-ship) A period in which a young person works with another person to learn a skill or trade.

bagwig (BAG-wig) A wig with the back hair enclosed in a small silk bag.

caul (KAWL) A net cap.

contract (KON-trakt) An official agreement between two or more people.

custom-made (KUS-tum-mayd) Made in a certain way.

dexterous (DEK-stuh-rus) Skillful with the hands.

dressed (DRESD) Arranged the hair by combing, brushing, or curling.

imported (im-PORT-ed) Brought from another country for sale or use.

journeyman (JER-nee-man) A worker who has learned a trade from one person, but who works for another.

penetrates (PEH-neh-trayts) Passes into or through.

pomade (poh-MAYD) A fragrant hair dressing.

status (STA-tus) Position or rank in relation to others.

tempered (TEM-perd) Brought to the desired hardness or strength by heating and cooling.

tone (TOHN) A shade of color.

weft (WEFT) Row of hair on a wig.

INDEX

WEBSITES

Due to the changing nature of Internet links, PowerKids Press has developed an online list of websites related to the subject of this book. This site is updated regularly. Please use this link to access the list:

www.powerkidslinks.com/jgca/wig/